START-UP▲
GUITAR

It's never been easier to start playing guitar!

Published by
Wise Publications
14-15 Berners Street, London W1T 3LJ, UK.

Exclusive Distributors:
Music Sales Limited
Distribution Centre, Newmarket Road, Bury St Edmunds, Suffolk IP33 3YB, UK.
Music Sales Pty Limited
20 Resolution Drive, Caringbah, NSW 2229, Australia.

Order No. AM1002903
ISBN: 978-1-84938-981-5
This book © Copyright 2011 Wise Publications, a division of Music Sales Limited.

Adapted by David Harrison from an original book by Artie Traum.
Produced by shedwork.com
Design by Fresh Lemon.
Photography by Matthew Ward.
Models: Sagat Guirey and David Weston.
Edited by Tom Farncombe.
Printed in the EU.

With thanks to the City Lit, London.

Your Guarantee of Quality
As publishers, we strive to produce every book to the highest commercial standards.
This book has been carefully designed to minimise awkward page turns and to make playing
from it a real pleasure. Particular care has been given to specifying acid-free, neutral-sized
paper made from pulps which have not been elemental chlorine bleached. This pulp is from
farmed sustainable forests and was produced with special regard for the environment.
Throughout, the printing and binding have been planned to ensure a sturdy, attractive
publication which should give years of enjoyment. If your copy fails to meet our high standards,
please inform us and we will gladly replace it.

www.musicsales.com

WISE PUBLICATIONS
part of The Music Sales Group
London / New York / Paris / Sydney / Copenhagen / Berlin / Madrid / Hong Kong / Tokyo

Playing a musical instrument is one of life's most rewarding pastimes and of all the instruments you could choose, the guitar might just be the most rewarding of all. Look at everything it has going for it: it's pretty easy to learn, it's portable, it's not too expensive, it sounds great, it comes in all shapes and sizes, and you can play virtually any kind of music on it, from classical to heavy metal!

If you're reading this and don't yet have a guitar, you're probably just about to get one.

The first question is 'which guitar?' Well, the truth is, as long as it works okay, any guitar will do when you're starting out, but it's a good idea to think about the style of music that you want to play, and choose a guitar accordingly.

You might want to take a trusted guitarist friend along to help you pick one out, but as long as you know your budget, have an idea of what sort you're after, and go to a reputable music store, you'll be fine.

CHOOSING A GUITAR

So what are the differences between the various kinds of guitar out there?

Steel String

The standard acoustic guitar sounds great without amplification—although many of them have a pickup built in, so you can put them through an amp for extra volume—and are traditionally played by folk-style guitarists. The steel strings give the guitar a 'twang' perfect for country and finger picking styles. However, they crop up all the time in rock and pop too.

It's a steel-string acoustic that you hear on early Bob Dylan records, 'Yesterday' by The Beatles and Oasis' 'Wonderwall'.

If you want a guitar you can take anywhere and play in lots of different styles, then this is the most obvious choice.

Tuning Peg

Headstock

Nut

Fret

Fingerboard Fretboard

Fret Marker

Fret Wire

Neck

Body

Soundhole

Saddle

Bridge

The steel-string guitar is the perfect instrument for acoustic styles, whether you're strumming or finger picking.

Classical

The classical guitar (below) is a bit more specialised. Its mellow sound is used in flamenco, Latin styles such as bossa-nova and rumba and various other ethnic styles—but it also appears in all sorts of pop, from The Beatles ('And I Love Her') to Sting ('Shape Of My Heart'). Of course, it's used for classical music too. The main difference to the steel-string acoustic is that the classical guitar's nylon strings are much gentler on the fingertips. That advantage is more-or-less balanced by the wider fingerboard, which some players find a bit of a stretch.

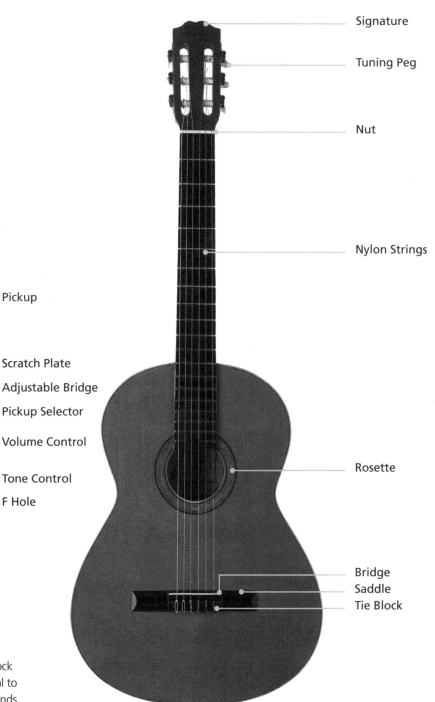

Signature

Tuning Peg

Nut

Nylon Strings

Pickup

Scratch Plate

Adjustable Bridge

Pickup Selector

Volume Control

Rosette

Tone Control

F Hole

Bridge
Saddle
Tie Block

Electric

The electric guitar (above) might instantly be associated with rock icons such as Jimi Hendrix, but amplified instruments are crucial to blues and jazz as well, and there is a vast range of possible sounds that you can achieve from the electric to suit many styles.
You will need an amp, and that's an added expense, but if you're serious about achieving a rock sound, then an electric guitar is probably for you. You'll add all sorts of effects pedals and other electronic gizmos to your arsenal as you begin to discover the world of amplified guitar, but a small practice amp is fine to start with.

If you're not familiar with the sound of the classical guitar, try listening to Rodrigo's 'Concierto De Aranjuez'.

GETTING STARTED

Once you've got a guitar, there are a few things to sort out: first of all, you'll need to find somewhere to practise.

In the next section we'll look at posture, but for now try to find a chair that's not too low—definitely not an armchair or couch—so you can just about place your feet on the floor. Some people like to use a bar stool with a foot rail.

Whatever chair you choose, you might well find that a strap helps to support the guitar, taking the strain off your arms.

A comfortable place to sit is a must, and a strap helps to take the weight off.

You'll also need a tuner: electronic tuners are cheap and easy to use, and very accurate. Some clip on to your guitar, and others can be put on a desk in front of you.

If you have an electric guitar, you'll probably need to plug the guitar into the tuner with a cable. We'll look at how to tune the guitar in a while.

There are a lot of other things you *could* buy at this point: picks and a capo for instance, but the only other thing you should really have is a spare set of strings.

They don't often break, but when they do, it's good to know that you have a replacement handy right away.

You should also have a music stand, and—to save your guitar from getting knocked over—a guitar stand.

Oh, and a nail file! Keep your left-hand fingernails short and clean and don't allow your right-hand fingernails to get too long or to split.

A stool like this is perfect for sitting to play the guitar.

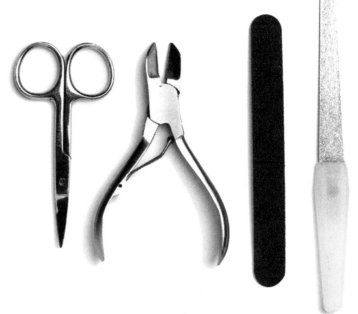

It's worth keeping a spare set of strings (above). Classical, electric and steel-string acoustic guitars require specific types of strings. Let your local music store recommend the right type for you.

Picks (below) are a good choice for strumming and picking to get a louder sound and to save your nails.

Carry a small selection of nailcare items in your case (above).

An electronic tuner is simple to use and very accurate (below).

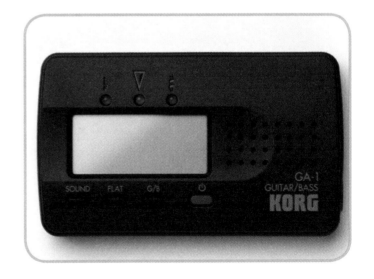

HOLDING THE GUITAR

Although the guitar is a folk instrument, and there are lots of opinions on the way it should be held, one thing is sure: it has to feel comfortable when you are playing.

You're bound to get a little tired, especially at the start, but having good technique will minimise any potential problems.

Sit with your feet flat on the floor, or upright on a stool, and perch a bit at the front of the seat.

The guitar should rest on your right thigh, and hopefully you'll find it more-or-less balances there with just a little help from your left hand, which lightly grips the neck.

The front of the guitar should face away from you so you can't see it if you look down.

Whether standing or sitting, the left-hand position is important. The thumb should stay behind the neck, positioned at about the 2nd fret, and the hand should form a gentle curve so that the fingers can come down onto the fretboard at right angles.

This way, you can be sure that the fingertips are making contact with just the strings they need to touch, and not getting in the way of any of the others.

A well-made guitar is balanced so that it should stay on your lap with the minimum of effort.

This means that your arms and hands will be free to concentrate on playing rather than holding the guitar tight.

Spend time experimenting with your guitar until you're able to keep it in position without thinking about it.

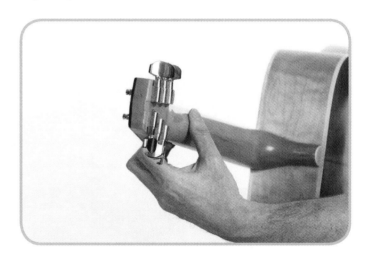

The right hand, whether strumming or picking, should hang loosely over the front of the guitar at the sound hole (if your guitar is acoustic) or the pickups (if it's an electric).

Make sure your body is relaxed, so you don't develop strains. If you feel any part of you getting sore, take a little rest and have a look to see whether you can change anything about the way you're holding the guitar that will help.

As you start to learn new chords, strumming techniques or anything else involving your hands, there will be a great temptation to look down at your hands to make sure they're in the right place.

But, since you shouldn't be able to see the front of the guitar if you're holding it right, you'd need to hunch right over or twist the guitar up towards you before you can see what you're doing. So get used to feeling for the right position with your fingers.

Try sitting with a mirror in front of you—even a make-up mirror placed on a desk or music stand should help. This way you can check your hand position without compromising your posture and technique.

With a music stand, any music books, song sheets or other paper can be held at eye level, and you should be able to keep a comfortable position for longer periods than if you had to keep looking down at your work.

TUNING

Getting the guitar in tune is a crucial skill. There are various methods, but they all involve adjusting the pitch of the open (unfretted) strings by turning the tuning pegs to tighten or loosen each string until it sounds the correct note. Let's look at the main methods.

Tuning the thicker strings can pull on the guitar neck enough to affect all the other strings, so there's no point in carefully tuning the thinner strings only to have to retune them once you've tuned the thicker ones.

Let's look at the sound source method first. These diagrams show the notes you need on the piano, the equivalent musical notation, and the appropriate strings on the guitar.

Notice how the strings are named (above right): the bottom string is the one that sounds lowest. The top string is the highest-sounding.

You can choose a sound source to tune against, such as a piano, pitch pipes, special audio tracks or a tuning fork; or else you can use an electronic tuner, which will tell you when your guitar is in tune.

Either way, you should start with the thickest (also known as the *bottom*, or *sixth*) string, and work your way through the strings to the thinnest (*top*, or *first*).

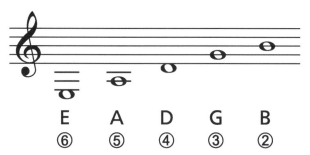

By the way: in guitar notation, notes are written an octave higher than the actual sounding pitch.

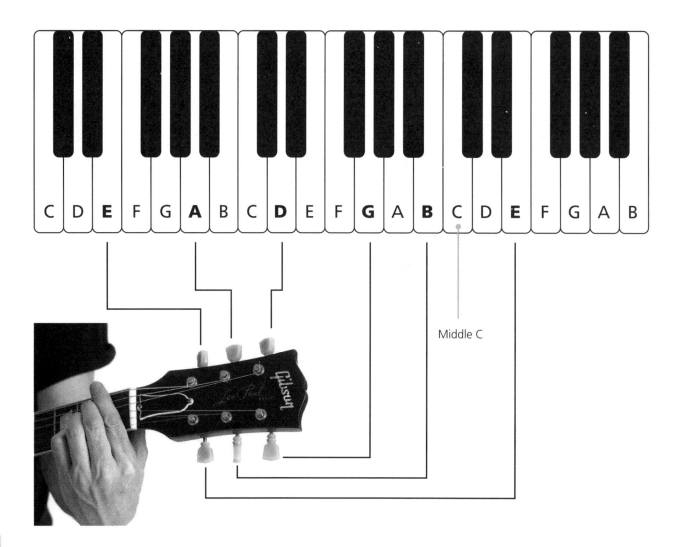

Middle C

Relative Tuning

If you tune the bottom string accurately, you can then use that string to tune the others.

Here's how it works:

- Place a finger on the 5th fret of the bottom (sixth) string—this will give you the note you need (A) to tune the open fifth string.

- Once that's done, play a note on the 5th fret of the fifth string. It'll be D, which is the note you need for the open fourth string.

- And again, play a note on the 5th fret of the fourth string to give you the note you need (G) for the open third string.

- Now the sequence changes: this time, play a note on the 4th fret of the third string to sound B, which is the correct note for the open second string.

- Finally, play a note on the 5th fret of the second string to sound E, which is the note you'll need to tune the top string.

Although it might seem a bit fiddly, this method is great for checking a single string if you're in the middle of playing, and since it relies on your ears it's great training too... check the diagram below for fret positions for each of the reference notes.

Clip-on style tuners are especially convenient (see the section on electronic tuners, below).

Electronic Tuners

Using an electronic tuner has lots of advantages: they're pretty fool-proof, and very precise.

And, if you're tuning in a noisy situation, plugging a tuner in or attaching it to the guitar means you can tune even if you can't hear the guitar properly.

Play the bottom string, and the device will show you on its display whether you're low or high.

Tune the string in the right direction and, when it's up to pitch, the display will let you know. Simply move on to the next string and so on, until the instrument is tuned.

PRACTICE

It's a good idea to get into a realistic practice routine right away. Practice is the key to improving on the guitar, but it can also be the source of much frustration.

Here are a few tips to help you practise more effectively:

- A little practice every day is much more valuable than a finger-numbing mammoth session once a week.

- Keep a check on your posture and technique, to avoid any niggles creeping into your playing.

- Start slowly and build up: there will be a little wear and tear on your fingers to begin with, and it will take a bit of time to build up the calluses on your left finger tips—it's easy to overdo it, especially at the beginning.

- Set a target for each practice session, and make it realistic. Some people keep a practice diary, making a note of things to try in the next session. It's a great way to record your progress.

- Set aside time to play for fun. Keep it separate from your practice time, but make sure you sit and strum once in a while for no particular reason: after all, it's why you're learning to play guitar!

Practising a little each day is the best way to build up your technique and confidence steadily.

READING CHORD DIAGRAMS

The first thing you'll learn to play on the guitar are chords, which are groups of notes strummed together. Chords are written down using chord diagrams, or chord *boxes*.

Here's how they look:

The thicker line at the top is the nut—the white bone or hard plastic piece at the top of the guitar neck.

The horizontal lines are frets—the wire divisions along the fingerboard.

The vertical lines are the strings, and the dark dots show where fingers are placed on the strings.

If an X appears above a string, this string shouldn't be played, and with an O, the string is played 'open': without any fingers on it.

Compare the top of the neck with the chord box

Here's how the chord boxes are used in this book—they are displayed upright, accompanied by a photograph of the fingers in a natural, horizontal position. Compare the diagram with the photograph to see how they relate.

Left-hander?

If you happen to be left-handed, there's nothing standing in your way to playing the guitar. There are plenty of left-handed guitars out there, and as you work through this book, you'll simply need to reverse everything you see.

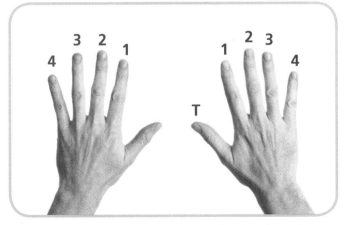

Guitarists number their fingers like so. T is for 'thumb', and although both hands are labelled the same way, the 4th finger of the right hand is hardly ever used.

Now you're ready to get playing. So let's have a look at your first chords.

YOUR FIRST TWO CHORDS

To start playing songs, you only need to know two chords, so let's make a start with A and E. Remember, the diagrams are shown upright, with the thick line at the top representing the nut—the piece at the top of the neck.

Try placing the 1st finger on the 2nd fret of the fourth string, like this:

Now, add the 2nd and 3rd fingers on the third and second strings, also on the 2nd fret, like so:

You're now fingering an A chord. If you brush down lightly across the strings with your right thumb, you'll hear the result. You may find that some of the notes are a bit muffled, so see if you can adjust the fingers until each note sounds out clearly.

You might need to ensure your thumb is in just the right place at the back of the neck to give your fingers the best possible chance of coming down onto the fingerboard at an angle approaching perpendicular: otherwise you risk touching more than one string with each finger.

We'll begin by taking a close look at the way a single finger should sit on the fretboard. The fingertip should come down at right angles to the fretboard onto the string just behind the fretwire. If you find you're struggling to make a note sound without a huge effort, go back and check this basic finger position (see below).

Press the strings down as near as you can to the fret without them actually being on the fret. If you're pressing very hard to get a clear sound, there might be something a bit wrong with your finger position, so stop again and check that.

Try to bring the fingertip down onto the string just behind the fretwire.

For now your right hand can simply curl up slightly and strum down across the strings. We'll get into some more advanced strumming soon, but for now just brush down with the thumb.

Brushing the strings with the thumb is a good way to hear how chords sound.

Give the A chord another go, and this time try to strum down without touching the bottom string. Ideally A doesn't use the bottom string, as you can see in the diagram.

Once you're happy with it (and it doesn't have to be perfect for now) we'll move on to our second chord, the chord of E.

E is a great chord for bringing out the full character of your guitar. It uses all six strings, and it looks like this:

Although it might not seem very helpful at the moment, make a note of the position of the 2nd and 3rd fingers relative to each other. They're next door to one another, just as they were for the A chord.

The fact is, playing chords on the guitar is easy enough: the challenge is often changing from one chord to another. Finding any similarities you can between chord shapes will give you a head start, and that's just what we're going to do now.

TOP TIP ✓

Changing from one chord shape to another is often more of a challenge than playing chord shapes on their own. Try to find any useful similarities between shapes to make the job easier.

CHORD CHANGES AND YOUR FIRST SONG

Take a look at this piece of music: it's
four 'bars' long, and alternates between
the chord of A and the chord of E.

Play the exercise slowly through, and
try to keep a steady beat.

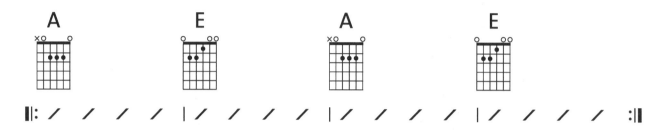

Strum down each time you see a slash (/). Each slash
represents a single beat of music.

Four strums of A will make a *bar*, and then it's time to play
a bar of E.

The first few times, you might prefer to strum once on A,
and count the four beats out while you change to E. Try to
play the E chord right at the beginning of the new bar.

Count again and change back to A, and so on. Once you
have done it several times, you'll be able to strum slowly
through, once on each beat without having to pause to
change the shapes.

Notice the double bar lines with dots:

These are repeat marks, and are found either side of a
repeated section of music. In this case, they indicate simply
that the whole of the music should be played again.

Check the chord diagram for A once more, and remember
not to play the bottom string when you strum. If you
happen to strum the bottom string too, it's not going
to sound too terrible on an A chord, but there are times
where it will sound messy and clash with the music.

Get into the habit of learning just which strings are needed
for each new chord you see, and spend a little while seeing
just how your strumming hand moves across the strings.

Eventually you'll be able to miss out the bottom string
without even thinking.

When you're reasonably happy with the way things are
going, you'll be ready to tackle your first song (opposite).

It uses both the chords you've just
been playing, A and E.

There are rhythm slashes as
before, and this time
arrows are added to
show you to strum
down on each beat.

You don't need to read music notation
to play the song on the next page: just
follow the strums for the chords and sing
the words.

If any of the songs in this book aren't
familiar to you, listen to some recordings
to learn the tune.

Try playing this gospel standard using the two chords. To start with, you might try just playing each chord once, clearly, when it appears, and count through until it's time to play the next new chord. As you play, let your ears help you to tell which chord to play.

Soon you'll start to predict when the new chord comes by the sound it should make.

Take the song slowly, and try to move smoothly between chords. Check that your fingers are making the most efficient and accurate movements possible.

As for the right hand, again the movement should be smooth and steady. It's enough just to stroke the strings gently with the thumb.

Down by the Riverside

Gon-na lay down my bur - den,_ down by the ri-ver- side,_

down by the ri-ver- side,_ down by the ri-ver- side._ Gon-na

lay down my bur - den,_ down by the ri-ver - side,_ and

stu - dy war no more._

STARTING TO PICK

Now that you've conquered your first song, let's look at a more interesting way to strum. In fact, you're going to strum and pick. Picking is an essential part of guitar technique, especially in **acoustic styles such as country and folk, and it's widely used in blues, ragtime and some types of jazz too, so it's worth spending some time on it.**

In this next exercise, the thumb is going to pick just the bottom string of the chord on the first beat, and again on the third beat. The lowest note of a chord is called the bass note. Now, the bass note of the A chord is on the fifth string, but on the E chord it's the sixth string.

Alternate the picked bass notes with strummed chords by brushing the strings down with the backs of the fingernails. Hold the hand loosely, and allow the nails to pass smoothly across the strings. The hand motion should come from the wrist, which should be relaxed.

On beats 2 and 4, strum the whole chord as before. Try this exercise, slowly and steadily at first:

Try to keep the rhythm steady and smooth.
Take it slowly at first, gradually increasing the tempo.

Now try the same thing on the E chord:

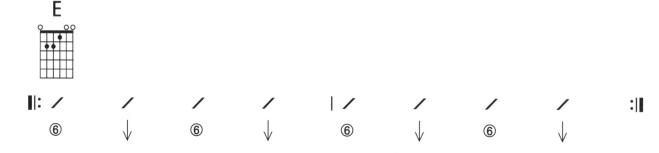

Once you are happy with the basic strum, you could try alternating between two bass notes on two different strings. Have a look at the next exercise (below).

This time, pick and strum the A chord as before, but alternate with the thumb between the fifth string and the sixth string. It'll create a rhythmic bass line in a country style reminiscent of the music of Johnny Cash.

> Try not to let each thumbed note ring out for more than one beat to keep the pattern sounding clean.

A

⑤ ↓ ⑥ ↓ ⑤ ↓ ⑥ ↓

Then try alternating the bass on the E chord. This time, pick the sixth string on the first beat, and change to the fifth string on the third beat. You'll achieve a similar sound to the previous exercise:

E

⑥ ↓ ⑤ ↓ ⑥ ↓ ⑤ ↓

Finally, let's try another chord shape.

This one goes well with A and E. It's the chord of D. It only uses four strings, so take care when strumming not to play the bottom two strings by mistake. Here it is:

If you like, you could try playing the alternating bass you just looked at. For D, you would alternate between the fourth and fifth strings:

D

 ④ ↓ ⑤ ↓ ④ ↓ ⑤ ↓

Down by the Riverside (complete)

Now that you know A, E and D, you can tackle the rest of 'Down by the Riverside'.

This time it's marked with the alternating bass strumming, too.

Gon-na lay down my bur - den,_ down by the ri-ver - side,_

down by the ri-ver - side,_ down by the ri-ver - side. Gon-na

lay down my bur - den,_ down by the ri-ver - side,_ and

stu - dy war no more._____ Ain't gon - na

Finish the song with three strums.

Here are three more songs that just use the chords of A, D and E. They'll give you a chance to practise changing between the chords and to pick & strum steadily.

Will the Circle Be Unbroken

Will the cir - cle be un - brok - en, by and by, Lord, by and by?_____ There's a bet - ter home a - - wait - ing in the sky, Lord, in the sky.

Finish this song with one strum, and let it ring for three beats.

The Banks of the Ohio

I asked my love to take a walk, Just a

lit - - tle way with me. And as we

walked a - long we talked All a -

- bout our wed-ding day.

'The Streets of Laredo' (opposite) has three beats to the bar, which creates quite a different feel.

Because there aren't an even number of beats, the *pick-strum, pick-strum* pattern won't work. So let's look at an alternative.

The simplest solution is to pick the bass note of the chord on the first beat as before, and strum the other two beats. This kind of rhythm is often referred to as 'boom ching ching' in folk and country circles:

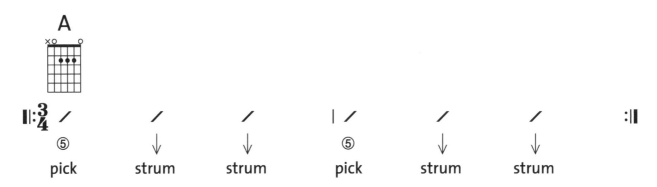

This will work fine for all three of our chords. Just remember to adjust the bass note picking for each chord: fifth string for A, fourth for D and sixth for E.

In cases where a chord lasts for more than one bar, you can alternate the bass note on the first beat of the subsequent bar:

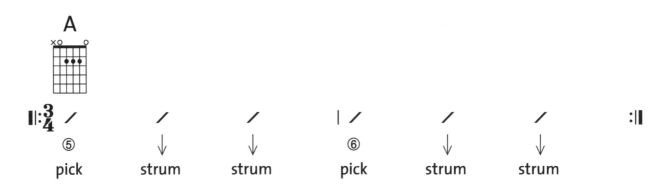

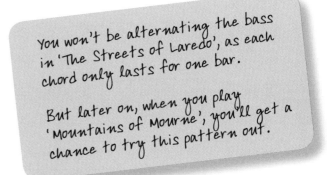

You won't be alternating the bass in 'The Streets of Laredo', as each chord only lasts for one bar.

But later on, when you play 'Mountains of Mourne', you'll get a chance to try this pattern out.

The Streets of Laredo

1. As I was a - walk - in' the streets of La - re - do, As
see by your out - fit that you are a cow - boy", these

I walked out in La - re - do one day, I
words he did say as I bold - ly walked by. "Come

spied a young cow - boy all wrapped in white lin - en, All
sit down be - side me and hear my sad sto - ry, I'm

wrapped in white lin - en and cold as they clay. 2. "I
shot in the breast and I know I must die".

TO PICK OR NOT TO PICK

Various guitar styles have traditionally been associated with different types of picks. Let's look at the main types.

The single, flat pick, usually called a *flatpick*, or *plectrum*, is widely used among both electric and acoustic guitarists. Many people like the crisp, bright sound they can achieve.

For harder rock lead lines with very light strings, a stiffer, thicker pick might be more suitable, while for strumming lightly on the relatively thick strings of a steel-string acoustic, a light, flexible pick is a better bet.

Jazz guitarists seem to like the small, hard plectrums that allow them to target strumming and lead lines.

Finger picking guitarists who need to pick several strings at once, on the other hand, often go for sets of metal or plastic picks that fit around the fingers and thumb.

Some people prefer to use their nails to pick and strum. If you plan to do this, it pays to carry a nail file and scissors with you to keep your nails in shape.

However, if you'd prefer to use a pick, there's a baffling array of different types available. None are expensive, so the best approach is probably just to buy a variety and try them out.

Below is a selection of different types.

A standard nylon pick is the type used by most people. A medium gauge of 0.6 mm is about average. Many guitarists will use a thicker pick on lighter strings, and a thinner pick on heavier strings.

A small, thick pick is the type favoured by many jazz guitarists.

Metal and plastic picks that fit directly onto the fingers are a specialist type used by finger picking guitarists in folk, blues and country styles.

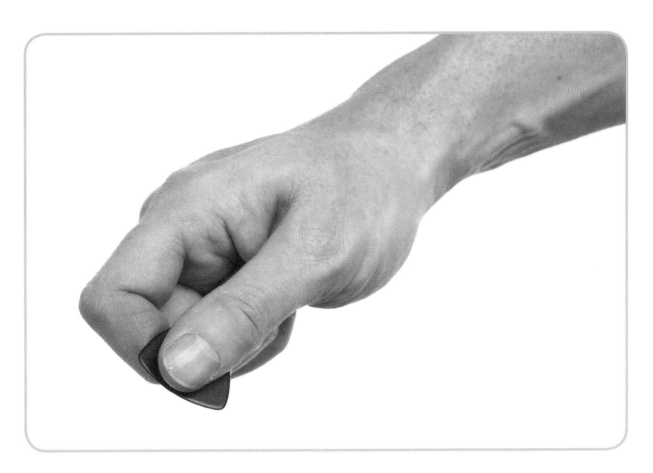

Now, get back to 'Will the Circle Be Unbroken' (page 22) and play it using a plectrum. Hold the pick between your right thumb and index finger—not too tight, but not too loose either. You want to exert a fair amount of pressure without overdoing it.

As you can see, only a small part of the pick should project beyond the edges of your thumb and finger. Your wrist should stay relaxed. To get the feeling, shake the pick as if you were shaking a thermometer.

Now, hit the fifth string while holding an A chord and strum down as you did before. Is the sound clean? Can you hear all of the notes? If the sound is muddy, don't despair. You will get the hang of the pick eventually, if you keep at it.

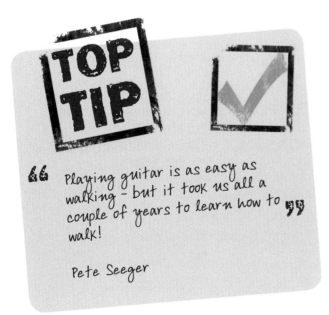

TOP TIP ✓

" Playing guitar is as easy as walking — but it took us all a couple of years to learn how to walk! "

Pete Seeger

RED RIVER VALLEY

Here's another new chord. It's a variation on the E shape we've already looked at, called E7. You can play it by taking a finger away from the E shape:

You could also try an optional extra note on the 2nd string:

For this song, we haven't included notation for the picking and strumming pattern.

Strum as before, with the optional alternating bass picking—but get used to playing the correct bass strings from memory: it'll stick in your mind much quicker that way.

Give it a go with this new song: it uses all the chords you've tried so far, and goes at a fairly brisk pace.

Try using all the alternating bass picking if you like, but you might need to play it through slowly a few times first to make a note of which bass notes to use.

The bass notes for E7 are the same as those for E.

In the second line, notice the change from E to E7: play the E shape, and then lift off the 2nd finger as you move to E7. You can alternate the bass in the same way for both chords, which will create continuity.

2.
Won't you think of this valley you're leaving,
Oh, how lonely, how sad it will be.
Oh, think of the fond heart you're breaking,
And the grief you are causing to me.

3.
From this valley they say you are going,
When you go, may your darling go to?
Would you leave her behind unprotected,
When she loves no other but you?

4.
I have promised you, darling, that never
Will a word from my lips cause you,
And my life, it will be yours for ever,
If you only will love me again.

Red River Valley

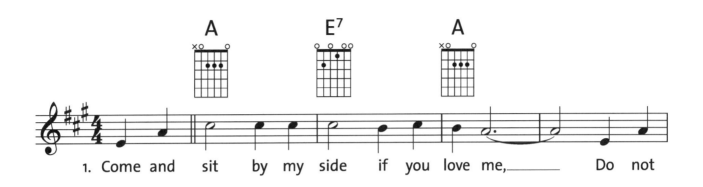

1. Come and sit by my side if you love me,_____ Do not

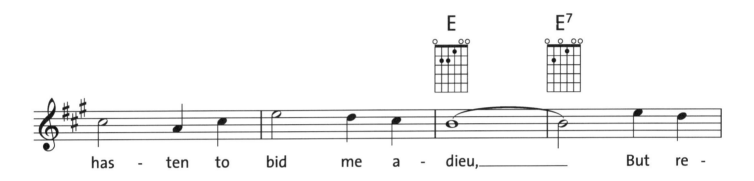

has - ten to bid me a - dieu,_____ But re -

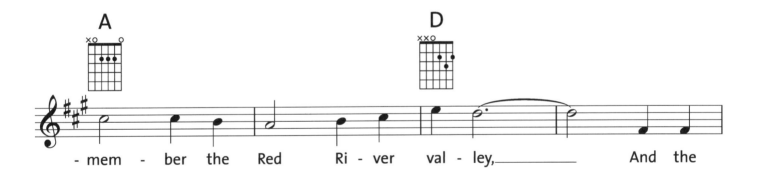

- mem - ber the Red Ri - ver val - ley,_____ And the

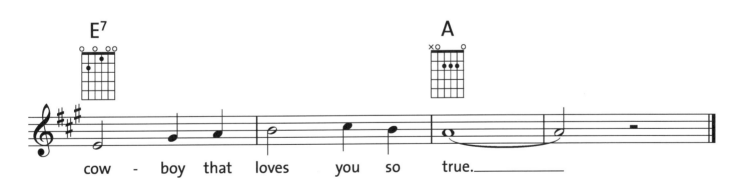

cow - boy that loves you so true._____

SHE'LL BE COMING 'ROUND THE MOUNTAIN

All the music we've played so far is in the key of A: hopefully you can hear how it comes to rest on the final A chord of the song each time. A, D and E, plus E7, are all you'll need to play countless songs in this key.

To play in other keys, you simply need to find similar groups of chords. Try these chords, to play in the key of D.

The new shape of G needs special care. You might find it easist to put the little finger into position first, then move the 2nd and 3rd fingers into place.

Practise moving from G to D and back again several times, and check that your thumb is sitting at the back of the neck to give your fingers the support they need.

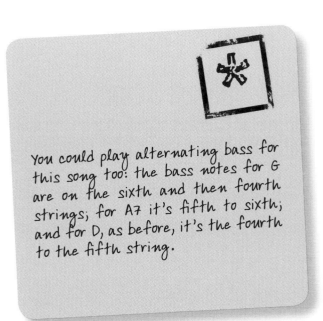

You could play alternating bass for this song too: the bass notes for G are on the sixth and then fourth strings; for A7 it's fifth to sixth; and for D, as before, it's the fourth to the fifth string.

2.
She'll be driving six white horses when she comes,
She'll be driving six white horses when she comes,
She'll be driving six white horses, driving six white horses,
She'll be driving six white horses when she comes.

3.
Oh, we'll all go out to meet her when she comes,
Oh, we'll all go out to meet her when she comes,
Oh, we'll all go out to meet her, all go out to meet her,
Oh, we'll all go out to meet her when she comes.

4.
She'll be wearing a blue bonnet when she comes,
She'll be wearing a blue bonnet when she comes,
She'll be wearing a blue bonnet, wearing a blue bonnet,
She'll be wearing a blue bonnet when she comes.

She'll be Coming 'Round the Mountain

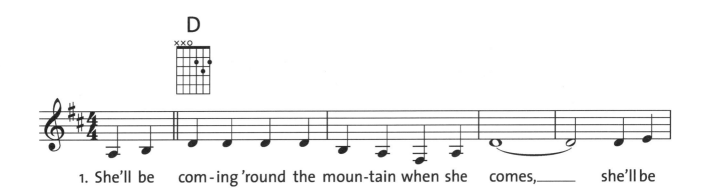

1. She'll be com-ing 'round the moun-tain when she comes,_____ she'll be

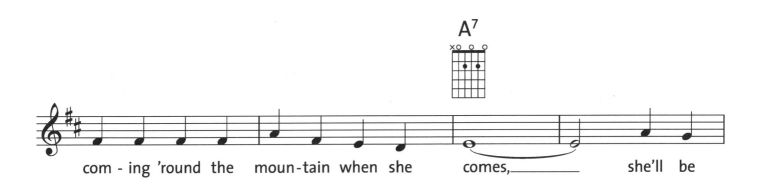

com - ing 'round the moun-tain when she comes,_____ she'll be

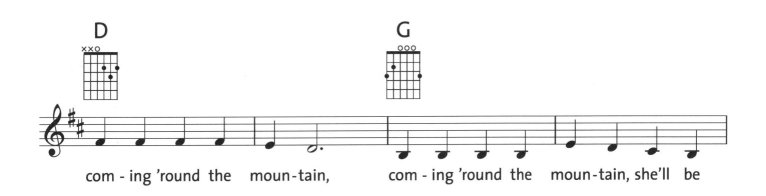

com - ing 'round the moun-tain, com - ing 'round the moun-tain, she'll be

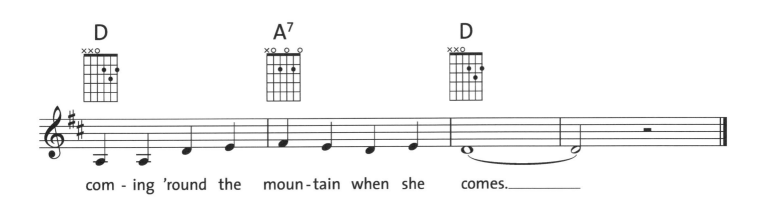

com - ing 'round the moun-tain when she comes._____

PLAYING IN MORE KEYS

Now here are some chords for the key of C.

For F, place the 1st finger across the 1st fret of both the first and second strings. This is known as a *barre*.

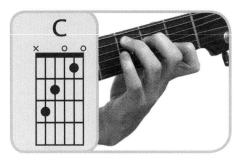

These chords, two of which we've already played, will give you a group for G:

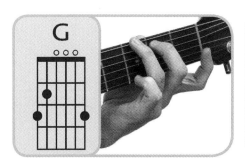

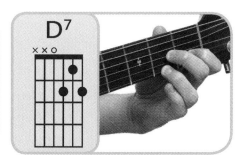

As you already know E and A, you only need one more chord to play in the key of E:

Alternate the bass for B7 as follows:

Play the standard bass note on the first beat. Then move the 2nd finger over to the 2nd fret of the bottom string, and play the new bass note on beat 3.

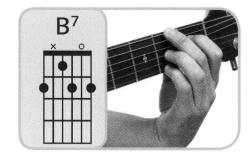

In the next song, strum down on the second and fourth beats as before, but this time follow it with an up-strum half a beat later, as shown. It'll create more rhythmic interest and help the song flow better.

If you're using a pick, hold it loosely and strum gently. If you're strumming with your fingers, the up-strums should be played with the back of the thumbnail, and the down-strums with the backs of the fingernails.

Mama Don't Allow

Ma-ma don't al-low no gui-tar play-in' round here.

Ma-ma don't al-low no gui-tar play-in' round here.

I don't care what Ma-ma don't al-low, gon-na pick my gui-tar, a - ny- how.

Ma-ma don't al-low no gui-tar_ play-in' round here.

MINOR CHORDS

Now it's time to try a new type of chord, the minor chord. Minor chords have a different sound, but are often used in combination with the ones we've already covered.

Minor chords are indicated by the letter 'm' after the chord name as shown below.

Try this chord sequence to hear how major and minor chords can be combined. This first example is in the key of C:

C   Am   Dm   G⁷

‖: / / / / | / / / / | / / / / | / / / / :‖

This sequence is used a lot in pop and rock, and was especially popular in rock 'n' roll ballads.

Now try it in G:

G   Em   Am   D⁷

‖: / / / / | / / / / | / / / / | / / / / :‖

Minor chords also crop up in sad blues songs like this next one. Strum each beat rhythmically and slowly, without alternating the bass picking.

St. James Infirmary Blues

MORE ALTERNATING BASS

The next song uses just two chords. For D minor, alternate the bass from the fouth string to the fifth.

For C, you'll need to move the 3rd finger down to the 3rd fret of the sixth string for the third beat, a little like the way the bass note changed for B7 in 'Mama Don't Allow' on page 33. This is shown in the two pictures on the right.

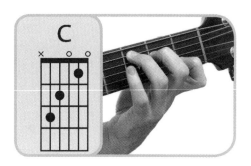

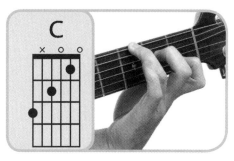

Play an alternating bass for the chord of C between the fifth and sixth strings on the 3rd fret.

Try alternating between the bass notes for each chord you know, and see if you can memorise which pairs of strings are required for each chord shape. Eventually, you'll see a pattern emerging:

4- or 5-string chords

On any chord where the bass note is on the fourth or fifth strings, alternate between the bass note and the note on the next string down, on the same fret (or open string).

Take a look at the chords of C, Am and D, for example, and check this pattern. It'll work for any major or minor chord, and should be very useful.

6-string chords

If you're playing a 6-string chord, it's likely either to be an E-type or a G-type.

- For G chords (G, G7 etc.) alternate from the sixth to the fourth strings.

- For E chords (E, Em, E7 etc.) alternate from the sixth to the fifth strings.

Drunken Sailor

READING TABLATURE

For strumming chords, diagrams showing left-hand finger positions are sufficient. But when it comes to finger picking, guitarists use a more complete notation system. This is tablature, or *tab*.

Tablature is a musical notation system for stringed instruments that shows the performer exactly where to play each note on the fretboard. This notation is used instead of standard notation, which shows the actual pitches.

If you haven't yet learned to read either system, you should try learning tablature first. It's easier to learn, and it's mandatory for much guitar music, especially for alternate tunings.

The tablature system consists of six horizontal lines, each representing a guitar string. The bass string is the bottom line of the tablature staff, and the treble string is the top line.

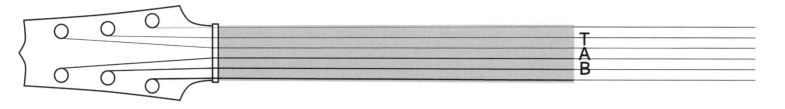

This layout is inverted from the actual string positions on the instrument. Here, the high-pitched notes lie high on the staff and the low-pitched notes lie low on the staff. In this way tablature resembles standard notation.

A number on a line indicates at which fret to depress that string. This example (right) describes all six strings of an E7 shape, picked in turn, starting with the lowest.

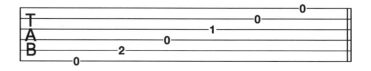

Sometimes, the stems and beams above or below the staff denote the rhythm. In this example, the rhythm is a series of eighth notes.

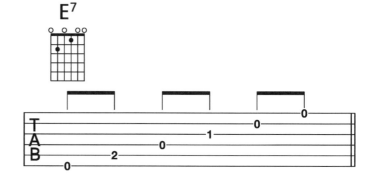

Where two or more notes are played simultaneously, they are
stacked up on the stave.

Compare these diagrams with the equivalent notes shown in tab
to see how this works.

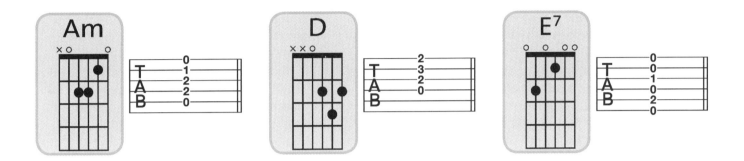

The next example shows notes of various chords played one after
the other. This type of pattern is known as an *arpeggio*. Compare
the chord diagrams with the notation, and pick the passage slowly
through until the arpeggios are smooth.

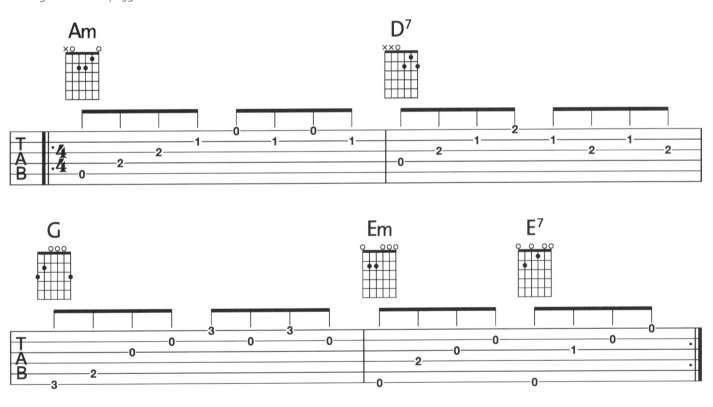

TOP
TIP

Remember: it can be more of a challenge
to play smoothly at a slower tempo,
because there's no chance of bluffing
your way through!

FINGER PICKING

To start with, you strummed all the notes of the chord at once. Then, we added picked bass notes. Now we'll play the notes of the chord individually to create finger picking patterns. Finger picking is perhaps the most satisfying of all guitar styles, and it is one of the most challenging to master.

There are endless ways to approach this technique: from the thumping blues of Robert Johnson, Skip James, and Ry Cooder; the subtle melodic ideas of Doc Watson and Chet Atkins; to the energetic, percussive pyrotechnics of Newton Faulkner and Tommy Emmanuel.

Your thumb is the pivot point of all finger picking. Let's build up a pattern little by little on an E chord. Eventually the pattern will require your right thumb, together with the 1st, 2nd and 3rd fingers.

The fingers will remain on the top three strings throughout, with the thumb moving to whichever string is needed for the correct bass note.

As you try these exercises, be sure to use the correct finger each time.

Start by slowly moving your thumb back and forth from the sixth string to the fifth string.

Give two beats to each bass note:

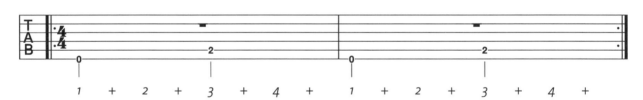

Now, add a note on the second string played at the same time as the bass notes—every two beats. Use your 2nd finger for these second-string notes:

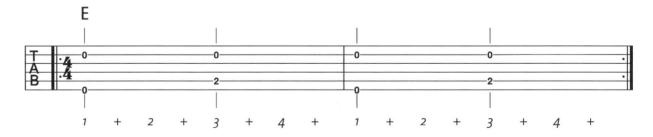

Next, add notes in between on the top string, with the 3rd finger. Play this through until it 'sits' in your fingers (ex. 3).

Count 'I and 2 and 3 and 4 and' as you start to play these exercises to keep the rhythm steady.

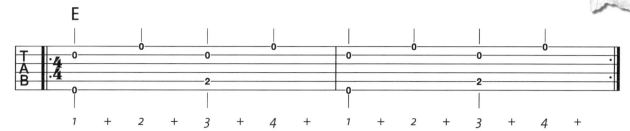

Try adding a note on the third string, played with the 1st finger, together with the 3rd-finger notes.

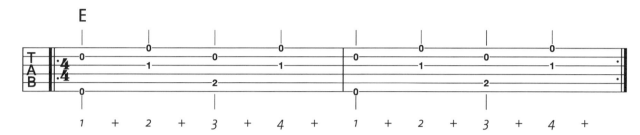

When that's smooth, move on to the next example. Here, the same notes are played, but the finger pattern is broken up over the thumb bass notes. This makes a great ragtime-style picking pattern:

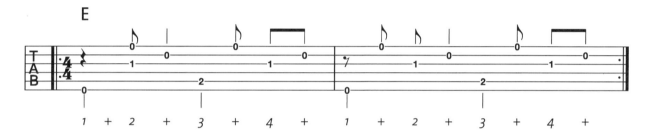

Experiment with different accents, and at different speeds. You'll be surprised how something as simple as changing the way the notes are accented can change the feel of the pattern. Finally, here's the same pattern on A and B7:

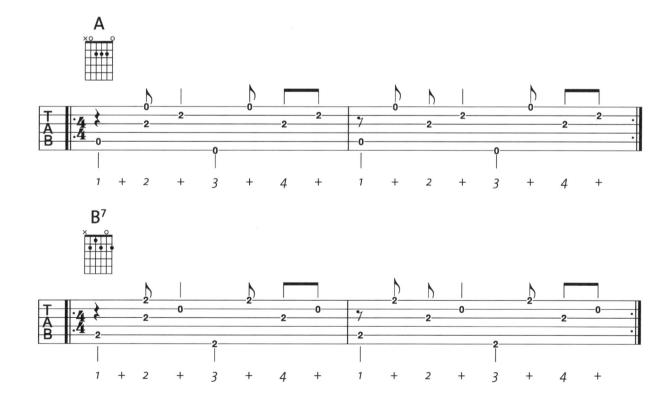

Once you're comfortable with this pattern, try it on songs throughout the book. Keep the fingers on the top three strings, and be sure to vary the bass notes (picked with the thumb) according to the different chords.

Feel free to experiment with strumming and picking patterns. You could even write down patterns that you particularly like.

PICKING IN 3/4

Like 'Streets of Laredo', this next song has three beats to the bar. Most chords last at least two bars each, so it's ideal for an alternating bass pattern like the one below.

If you're not sure how to alternate some of the bass notes, take another look at bottom of page 36, which gives you the 'rules' for alternating bass.

The song splits into two sections: try picking the first part, and strumming the second part for contrast.

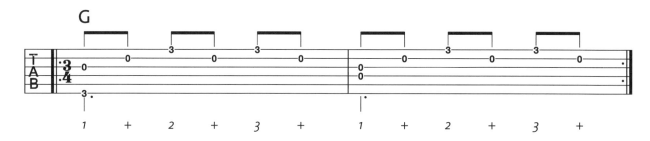

Mountains of Mourne

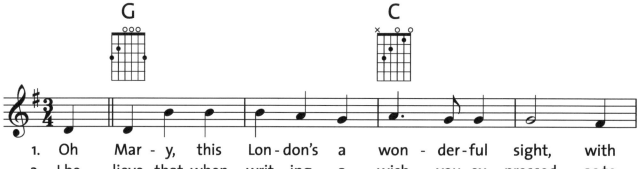

1. Oh Mar - y, this Lon - don's a won - der - ful sight, with
2. I be - lieve that when writ - ing a wish you ex - pressed as to
3. There's beau - ti - ful girls here, oh nev - er you mind, with

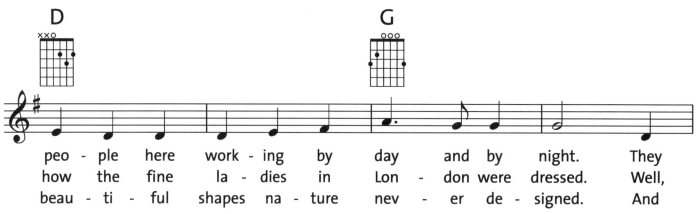

peo - ple here work - ing by day and by night. They
how the fine la - dies in Lon - don were dressed. Well,
beau - ti - ful shapes na - ture nev - er de - signed. And

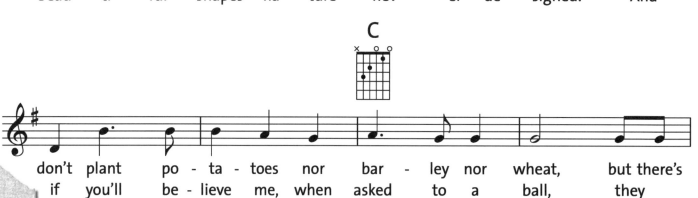

don't plant po - ta - toes nor bar - ley nor wheat, but there's
if you'll be - lieve me, when asked to a ball, they
love - ly com - plex - ions all ros - es and cream, but

MORE SONGS

1. I woke up this morn-ing with an aw-ful ach-ing head._____ I woke

up this morn-ing with an aw-ful ach-ing head._____ My

new man had left me just a room and an emp-ty bed._____

2.
He's a coffee grinder—grinding all the time
He's a coffee grinder—grinding all the time
He can grind my coffee, 'cause he's got a brand-new grind.

3.
If you get good loving, never go and spread the news
If you get good loving, never go and spread the news
Gals will double-cross you and leave you with the empty bed blues.

Using the picking pattern on page 41, try accenting some of the off-beat notes to create a syncopated feel, in the style of a ragtime beat: and, like a rag, it shouldn't be played too fast...

Freight Train

1. Freight train, freight train run so fast,___

Freight train, freight train run so fast.___

Please don't tell what___ train I'm on,___ They won't

know what___ route I've gone._____

2.
When I'm dead and in my grave,
No more good times will I crave.
Place the stones at my head and feet,
And tell them all that I've gone to sleep.

3.
When I die, Lord, bury me deep,
Way down on old Chestnut Street,
So I can hear old Number Nine
As she comes rolling by.

The change from G – B7 – C might take some practice, but stick with it, as it's a great sound!

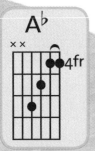

A♭

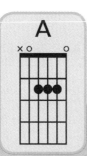

A

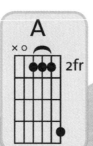

A

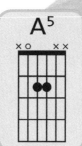

A⁵

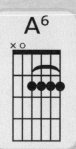

A⁶

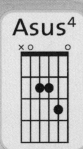

Asus⁴

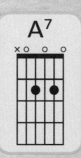

A⁷

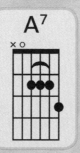

A⁷

A⁷sus⁴

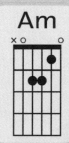

Am

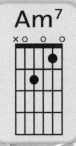

Am⁷

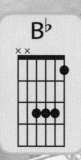

B♭

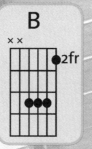

B

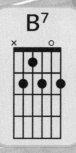

B⁷

Bm

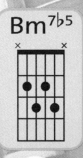

Bm⁷♭⁵

C

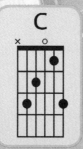

C

Cmaj⁷

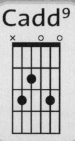

Cadd⁹

C⁷

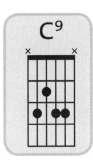
C⁹

Caug

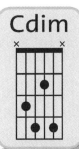
Cdim

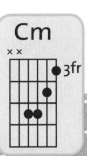
Cm

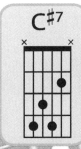
C♯⁷

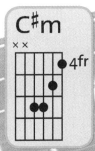
C♯m

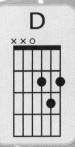
D

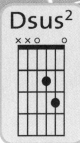
Dsus²

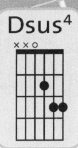
Dsus⁴

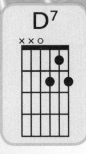
D⁷

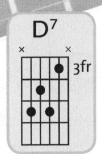
D⁷

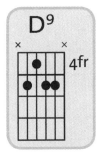
D⁹

Dm

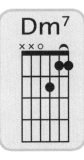
Dm⁷

D♯dim

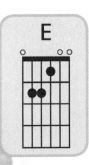
E

Esus⁴

E⁵

E⁷

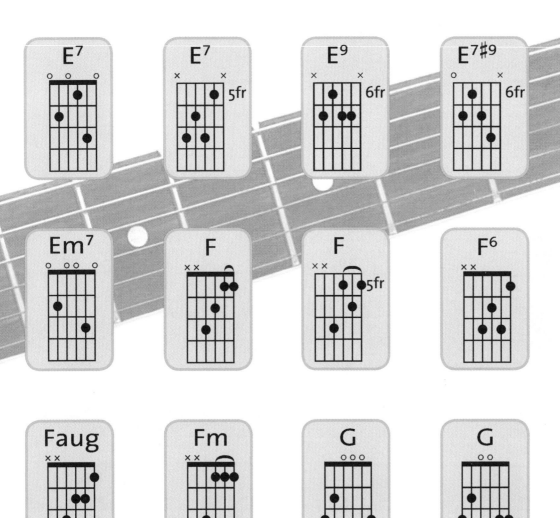

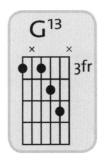

3456789